W9-CFL-600

COCKATIELS
AS A NEW PET

JOHN COBORN

CONTENTS

Photos by Dr. Gerald E. Allen, Glen S. Axelrod, Horst Bielfeld, Cliff Bickford, Rebecca Brega, Michael Gilroy, E. Goldfinger, Bruce D. Lavoy, Horst Mueller, N. Richmond, San Diego Zoo, T. Tilford, Wayne Wallace, Louise Van der Meid, Vogelpark Walsrode, R. Williams.

T.F.H. Publications, Inc.
One TFH Plaza
Third and Union Avenues
Neptune City, NJ 07753

This book has been published with the intent to provide accurate and authoritative information in regard to the subject matter within. While every precaution has been taken in preparation of this book, the publisher and author assume no responsibility for errors or omissions. Neither is any liability assumed for damages resulting from the use of the information herein.

ISBN 0-86622-612-5

www.tfh.com

Introduction

Next to the budgerigar and the canary, the cockatiel is probably the world's most popular cage or aviary bird. There are many reasons for this, the least of which must be this little parrot's charming temperament, its ability to mimic the human voice, its availability in a variety of attractive colors and most importantly, its readiness to breed in captivity—even in the most confined of accommodations. In addition, it does not have the rasping, raucous voice of many other parrots; it readily becomes finger-tame, is relatively intelligent and is entirely suitable for the beginner, whether he requires a single pet bird in a cage as a companion, or wishes to try his hand at color breeding.

Throughout the ages, people have kept birds in cages. In fact, man has probably done this since before he was able to write about it. We do know, from ancient signs and documents of many civilizations, that birds have been kept for various reasons. Apart from their being of economic importance, such as domestic fowl, the major motives for keeping birds seem to have been their esthetic appeal. The early Orientals have left

Cockatiels are second only to budgerigars in parrot popularity; in personality they are second to none.

2

The cockatiel has been around in captivity long enough to be considered completely domesticated—and some birds have even taken control of the house!

behind a wealth of colorful bird representations, depicted on silks, porcelain and other articles, indicating that bird-keeping was not unknown to them. The ancient Egyptians made references to ducks, ibis, parrots and pigeons in their hieroglyphics and the South American Incas were known to have tamed species such as Amazon parrots and macaws. Primitive tribes today still keep various bird species as household pets.

And so the science of aviculture developed. It gives people the opportunity to observe birds at close quarters without the necessity to seek out wild habitats. It enables them to enjoy the brilliant colors, the lively songs, the amusing antics and the often bizarre appearance, without having to leave home. As civilization developed, so did aviculture. Today, our knowledge of the biology of many bird species makes it relatively easy to provide captive conditions which resemble or at least substitute those found in the wild habitat. Birds given such conditions will soon feel comfortable and at ease in the captive environment, showing themselves at their finest.

Over the centuries many bird species have become domesticated. The domestic fowl, thought to be descended from the red jungle fowl, *Gallus gallus,* was probably kept in India as long as 5000 years ago. From there it has spread to all parts of the world and many varieties, some of which bear little resemblance to their wild ancestors, have been produced. Other birds—ducks, geese, turkeys, and pheasants for example— have also been cultivated, chiefly for reasons of economy; others, such as racing and homing pigeons, for their sporting qualities. It is somewhat surprising however, that certain birds have become domesticated, purely through their suitability as pets. These include the canary, the zebra finch, the society or Bengalese finch and the budgerigar, all of which appear now in many color varieties.

The cockatiel can be said to be almost completely domesticated. Breeding presents no particular problems and there are many mutant strains, making it a highly desirable subject for the color breeder, as well as the pet keeper. Many generations of captive breeding have produced color varieties to interest all bird lovers.

This little book has been written to introduce the newcomer to the cockatiel and, whether he wants to keep a single bird as a pet or have a garden aviary containing a colony of breeding pairs, the guidelines given here will enable him to purchase, house, feed, maintain, and breed these charming birds. It is sincerely hoped that the information herein will lead the prospective cockatiel enthusiast and family into many years of the pleasure and interest that aviculture can provide.

Opposite: Lovely lutino cockatiel. The pet cockatiel provides affection and companionship for young and old people alike.

4

Natural History

Cockatiels belong to the order of parrots, Psittaciformes, which includes parrots, macaws, cockatoos, lories, and parakeets. In the order there are seven families, about 77 genera and some 328 species, with a pantropical distribution, but they are particularly numerous in Australasia. Although having instantly recognizable general features, the parrot-like birds vary in size from the diminutive pigmy parrots, *Micropsitta* species, which at 10cm (4 in) are smaller than sparrows, to the relatively giant hyacinthine macaw, *Anodorhynchus hyacinthinus*, which may reach an overall length of 100cm (39 in).

Most species of parrot are brightly colored, are excellent mimics of the human voice (and other sounds) and are relatively intelligent—all factors which make many species highly desirable as household pets. Although differing widely in color and size, parrots have many anatomical features in common. A major characteristic is the robust beak, which reminds one of that of a bird of prey. The beak of a parrot is, however, set higher, is shorter and more curved than that of the raptor. The upper mandible curves down sharply over

Cockatiels are closely related to the cockatoos, which have many common features but are much larger birds.

6

The cockatiel's feet are zygodactylous, which means that two toes point forward and two point backward.

the lower and is provided with a series of horizontal grooves which not only help the bird 'manipulate' seeds, but also play a part in keeping the front of the lower mandible sharp. The tongue of most species is large and fleshy and is used to manipulate seed into a convenient position for de-husking. Some species, such as the lorikeets, have a brush-tongue, designed to remove nectar from flowers.

All parrots have zygodactylous feet; that is, they have two toes pointing forward and two to the rear. They share this phenomenon only with the order Cuculiformes and it is unlike the toe arrangement of any other group of birds, most of which have three toes pointing forward and one to the rear. This toe arrangement gives parrots unique gripping power which enables them not only to walk around efficiently in the branches of trees, but it enables most species to pick up food items and hold them to their beaks.

The cockatiel forms the single species *Nymphicus hollandicus*, placed in its own subfamily (Nymphicinae). So far, there have been no distinct geographical races (subspecies) described, but several field ornithologists have remarked on apparent differences in plumage pattern in various parts of the huge range of these birds.

The cockatiel is a common bird in much of inland Australia, especially in open or lightly timbered country. It is particularly numerous in the mid-north, where it is nomadic. It is absent from the extreme north (including the northern Kimberleys and the Cape York Peninsula), most of the coastal strip east of the Great Dividing Range and Tasmania. In the south, it is migratory, arriving in Victoria, New South Wales, and the southern parts of South and Western Australia in the spring and returning northward in the late summer and fall.

The average wild cockatiel is 32cm (about 12.5 in) in length, including the long pointed tail. The general plumage of the male is deep gray, the underparts lighter and often tinged with fawn. The forehead, cheeks, and throat are lemon-yellow, bordered with white. The narrow, erectile crest is gray, tinged with mustard-yellow, and the ear coverts are orange. A large white patch extends across the wing coverts to the inner flight feathers. The rump and upper tail feathers are paler gray, while the outer tail feathers are dark gray. The eyes are dark brown and the bill, cere, legs, and feet are gray.

The female is generally similar to the male, but often more slimly built with a narrower head. The forehead, cheeks, throat, and crest are gray, tinged with yellow, the ear coverts a duller orange. The ventral region and underside of the tail are marked with narrow, dull-yellow bands. The outermost tail feathers are yellow, banded with dark gray. Immature specimens are all similar to females and it is

In Australia, the cockatiel is often known as a "quarrion." This bird is a lutino.

somewhat difficult to distinguish the sexes until after the second molt, although in male specimens the head tends to be more robust and becomes progressively brighter yellow as the bird matures.

In the southern part of its range, the cockatiel breeds from August to December and in the north from April to August, though in some areas it may breed at almost any time of the year in favorable conditions. They nest in tree hollows, almost invariably near water, sometimes in trees partially submerged by flood waters. They may nest from 1-8m (3-25 ft) above the ground, depending upon available nesting sites. Two to eight white eggs about 2.5cm in width (1 in x 0.75 in) are laid, and these are incubated by both sexes, hatching in 18-20 days. The hatchlings are covered in a wispy, yellow down and take four to five weeks to fledge. They are fed by both parents.

Outside the breeding season, cockatiels are communal, congregating in flocks of several hundreds. They roost communally in trees or even on telephone wires. They are mainly seed eaters, foraging on the ground during the day for the seeds of grasses and other plants. They are particularly fond of the flowers and seeds of *Acacia* species. In some areas they are considered serious pests to cultivated crops and organized culling may take place when their numbers become too great.

Although household cockatiels are family favorites, wild cockatiels are often considered agricultural pests.

9

Cages

Cockatiels are suitable for keeping singly as pet birds, or a very fine display collection can be kept in an aviary. They are possibly the least aggressive of the parrot-like birds and can usually be kept with other bird species, even those which are much smaller than the cockatiels themselves. The following text discusses various types of cages and aviaries to suit the requirements of most prospective cockatiel keepers, whether intending to keep a single pet bird, a breeding colony, or separate pairs of birds for selective breeding.

The Pet Cockatiel Cage

For those who wish to tame and train a pet cockatiel, there are some very attractive small parrot cages on the market. They are usually constructed from stout, welded, chromium-plated or stainless-steel wire and mounted on a metal or

tough plastic base. The upper portion of the cage is attached to the base with clips, so that the parts can be easily separated at cleaning time. A ring is usually attached to the top of the cage, so that it may be suspended from a special stand (which may also be purchased) or from a ceiling hook. Alternatively, the cage can be simply placed on a

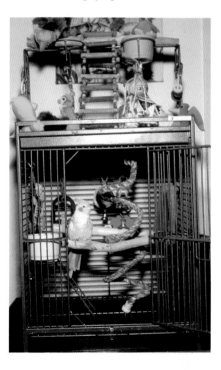

Pet stores everywhere carry an assortment of cockatiel cages. There are many models to choose from that will suit the exercise needs of your bird and fit your budget.

Your local pet shop can provide you with all the necessary cages, equipment, and food your bird will need.

flat surface, such as a table or a shelf. Cages are available in many shapes and sizes; they may be square, rectangular or circular-based, but the minimum cage size for a cockatiel should be not less than 50cm (20 in) in diameter and 70cm (27 in) tall. A square or rectangular-based cage is preferable to a circular one, as it allows that extra amount of volume. The practice of keeping a cockatiel in a cage designed for a budgerigar or a canary should be avoided, bearing in mind that our pet is at least double the size of these other birds.

New cages are usually purchased complete with all the accessories required for your bird's comfort. There may be two or more perches, which are placed horizontally across the cage at differing heights. These should be affixed as far apart as possible to allow maximum exercise as the bird moves from one to the other, but not so close to the cage wire that it becomes fouled with droppings. In addition a swinging perch is often included, this being suspended from the top of the cage; it will provide additional exercise for the bird and help alleviate boredom. Perches should preferably be of differing thicknesses so that the bird

11

can exercise its feet adequately and help prevent overgrown toenails. Perches may be manufactured from hardwood or plastic; softwood perches are virtually useless as the bird will soon chew these up. Hardwood is preferable to plastic as it is more natural and, although a determined bird may eventually chew it up, it will last much longer than softwood and can be easily replaced.

If you have a persistent perch chewer, you can divert him from this by giving him a natural perch at regular intervals. This consists of a thick twig from a non-poisonous tree or shrub. Should you be unsure of the nature of a certain tree, do not use it but use twigs from oak, beech, or known fruit trees (apple, plum, etc.) which have not been sprayed with insecticide or pesticide. The twig may be jammed across the width of the cage and the bird will have great fun clambering on it and stripping off the bark; if some of the bark is eaten, all the better, as it will contain valuable trace elements.

Food and water hoppers are also provided with the cages. These may be made from plastic, glass or stainless steel and are clipped into special spaces in the cage wire. They are so fashioned that they can be removed, cleaned, and replenished from outside the cage, without the necessity of disturbing the bird.

Some kind of replaceable floor covering must be used in the cage to prevent the base from becoming unpleasantly caked with dried bird droppings. Either bird sand or floor paper is usually used. The former can be sprinkled liberally over the floor of the cage and has several advantages. Good quality bird sand contains pieces of grit and trace elements which the bird may pick up to aid its digestion; it is also absorbent and will soak up bird droppings or water which is accidentally spilled from the hopper. Floor paper, which is just like abrasive sandpaper in appearance, can be made to fit exactly in the floor of the cage; advantages of this kind of floor covering are that it is easy to change when it becomes soiled and you will not get sand all over the floor when the bird flutters

Natural branches make wonderful perches for cockatiels. Be sure, however, that all branches placed in the cage have never been treated with pesticides or any other dangerous chemicals.

If you plan to keep two cockatiels together, the cage must be proportionally larger than that for a single bird.

about. However, some cockatiels will delight in tearing the paper into little pieces and it will be necessary to provide grit separately. Whatever kind of floor covering you use, it should be renewed daily and the cage base should be washed with soapy water, rinsed and dried. You can carefully remove the cage top while the bird is sitting on the perch, and place it temporarily over a sheet of newspaper while cleaning is in progress.

The siting of a cage in the home requires careful consideration. It is best to place the cage near a wall, so that members of the family are not likely to move on all sides of it. This will give a new bird in particular a greater feeling of security as soon as he knows there is a direction from which no "danger" is likely to approach. Cages should be located out of drafts but, at the same time, the area should be reasonably ventilated. Although cockatiels are fond of sunlight, they should never be placed in a position where they will receive direct sun rays through glass as this can cause rapid overheating (heat exhaustion). At the same time, however, all birds will appreciate some fresh air, so the cage may be placed in half shade near an open window or on a balcony when the weather is suitable.

Never place the cage in direct line of a television tube as there is a theory that cathode rays could have harmful effects on birds. If you want to watch TV late at night, it would be best to cover the cage with a cloth so that the bird can get undisturbed rest.

Breeding Cages

If bred on the colony system, cockatiels are most likely to be kept in aviaries. However, if selective color breeding is contemplated, the best results will be obtained if the birds are kept in individual pairs in special breeding cages. A breeding cage should be a minimum of 100 x 60 x 70cm (39 x 24 x 28 in) (the last measurement given is the height, which should be slightly more than the

breadth). The main structure of the cage is usually of plywood and is enclosed on all sides, with the exception of the front, which consists of a chromium plated or stainless steel grille. The grille contains one or more sliding or hinged doors; the latter, with a secure catch, are probably more suitable for cockatiels, which have an uncanny talent for learning to slide the former open! There should also be a facility for affixing food and water dispensers to the cage front. Many pet shops sell a

Many cockatiel owners take up the challenge of breeding for color. This is a pied cockatiel.

15

variety of unpainted cages of various sizes, complete with fronts. Alternatively, after ascertaining what size front grilles are available, the do-it-yourselfer can construct his own cage. Good quality exterior grade plywood about 12mm (.5 in) thick is probably the best (and easiest) material to use. Carefully work out the sizes required for the roof, the base, the ends, and the back (the latter can be made from thinner, 6mm or .25 in, plywood or hardboard, to reduce overall weight). Do not forget to include the thicknesses of the wood where the edges overlap! Many do-it-yourself stores have facilities for cutting plywood accurately to size. The timber is simply glued and tacked together to produce a strong, box-like cage, to which the front grille is attached with brackets (the grille should be secure, but easily removable if necessary).

To facilitate cleaning, it is advisable to have a sliding floor tray in the base of the cage so a space should be left below the grille for this purpose. The tray may be manufactured from thin

plywood, sheet aluminum, or plastic (the latter of appropriate size may be obtainable from your supplier). Whether you buy an unpainted cage or construct your own, it is advisable to treat the timber with a good primer, undercoat and topcoat of paint. The inside of the cage may be painted with non-toxic emulsion, preferably of a light color so that more light is reflected. The outer parts of the cage may be stained or just clear varnished; alternatively a coat of non-toxic gloss paint may be given. Of course, the

paint must be thoroughly dried out (give it a couple of days) before any birds are introduced. So that more volume is available inside the cage for the birds to move about, the nest box is best mounted on the outside, the birds gaining entrance to it through a 7.5cm (3 in) hole in the cage wall. A 7.5cm (3 in) perch is affixed to the wall just below the nest hole so that the birds will have comfortable access.

Taming and Training

This chapter is designed to meet the needs of those who wish to keep a pet cockatiel. Next to the budgerigar and the canary, the cockatiel is one of the world's most popular cage birds. It tames readily and, although not as vociferous as some of the parrots or the mynah bird, it can, in most cases, be taught to repeat a fair number of words and phrases, as well as mimic other sounds and whistle simple tunes.

If you want a talking cockatiel, it is best to obtain a specimen which has just left the nest but is able to feed itself. While cock birds are usually preferred as pets, it is difficult to distinguish the sexes at this young age and you may have to rely on the expert opinion of the breeder or dealer from whom you are purchasing it. Some dealers will offer a kind of guarantee that if the bird turns out to be a hen, he will exchange it. This is not to say that hens are not good pet birds; indeed, many people who start off with a hen become so attached to it that they would not change it for the world. Hens can be just as adept at learning to talk as cocks; they are just a little less colorful. Whether a bird turns out to be a good, mediocre or poor mimic is a matter of pure luck and has nothing to do with its color or its sex. In some ways they

Cockatiels enjoy all types of treats that are offered to them. Your local pet store will carry an assortment of treats that prove to be both nutritious and fun for the bird.

18

You can train your cockatiel to step up onto your shoulder or finger. Be patient when training your pet.

are just like humans, having degrees of ability and mood which depend on the individual. However, do not be discouraged by this; nearly all cockatiels become tame and trusting and will learn at least a few words.

Having brought your new pet safely home, he (the word "he" will be used here as a convenience; it can just as easily be "she") should be immediately placed in his cage, which you should previously have prepared and placed in the position it is to stay in. The door of the cage should be opened and the lid of the travelling box placed against it. Quickly open the lid and the bird should make its way into the cage. If he is reluctant to leave the travelling box, poke a pencil or similar object through one of the ventilation holes and *gently* push him towards the exit.

This move to a new home is one of the most (if not the most) traumatic times your bird will have to contend with. So you must be very gentle with him at first. Do not allow other pets such as dogs or cats to frighten him; nor allow boisterous children to run around the cage shouting their heads off. The

19

first few days will determine whether your bird is going to remain nervous and fearful of people, or become one of the family.

Keep a close eye on the bird for the first few hours and ensure that he can find his food and water dishes. Remember that the new surroundings will be very strange for him, and it will take him time to orientate himself. If possible, he should be placed in his new home in the morning, so that he has all day to adjust. If the bird does not feed from the dish in the first couple of hours (you can tell by the presence of seed husks in the dish or on the cage floor), sprinkle some seed on the floor of the cage.

Taming

For the first 24 hours, the bird should be left in peace and movements around him should be kept to a minimum. After this, no time is too soon to start taming him. Having chosen his name (which should be reasonably short and easily repeated, such as Peter, Cocky or Billy and *not* long and cumbersome like Napoleon or

Nebuchadnezzar), this should be the first word he is taught. Talk to the bird quietly and reassuringly every time you go near his cage, especially when you are about to clean the cage, or replenish food and water. His name should be uttered slowly and clearly as often as possible but with a pause between each utterance (for example: not Bobby, Bobby, Bobby, but Bobby; Bobby, Bobby!).

Give him a couple of days of just talking to him before you attempt to hand train him. Then, each time you are dealing with him, *very slowly* put your hand through the cage door and move it towards him. The moment he shows panic, you should freeze your movement until he has settled again. Then move slowly nearer to him, with the index finger stretched out. If he shows signs of panic again, slowly remove your hand and wait for a while before starting again. All the time you are doing this, speak to him in a soft reassuring voice, continually repeating his name.

Eventually he will allow you to touch the lower part

of his breast, which you should stroke with your index finger. After he allows you to do this a few times, place your index finger at the base of his breast, near to his feet and push gently, as though you are going to push him off his perch. With luck, he should step onto your finger and use it as a perch. Allow him to sit on your finger in the cage several times before attempting to remove him from the cage. Get him used to your movements by moving your hand slowly up and down or from side to side while he is sitting on your finger. At first he may have the odd moment of panic, as he will be mistrustful about your intentions (or at least the intentions of your hand, which he will probably regard as some entity in itself). When he is used to sitting on your finger for long periods, you can remove him slowly from his cage.

At this point, it is worth discussing the various dangers that can befall a cockatiel when he has free access to the living room. All caged cockatiels should

A fully flighted cockatiel should never be let loose outdoors. Such a bird is an escape waiting to happen even if he has been with you for years.

be given the opportunity of free flight in a room at regular intervals, so that they are able to exercise their wings. Before allowing the bird to leave his cage, ensure that all windows and doors are closed. Even a tame cockatiel, should he escape into the great outdoors, will become confused and frightened and it will be very difficult to catch him again—so it is better to be safe than sorry. It is best to

Pearl cockatiel. Many owners start taming by having the bird climb onto a stick, while others start right out using a finger.

lips at the prospect of a fat cockatiel on the menu! A friend of the author's allowed her "gentle" German Shepherd Dog to stay in the room once, when she let her "Clarence" out. At first the dog pretended to take no notice of the bird, apart from the movements of his eyes as the bird moved around the room. As soon as Clarence landed on the floor within striking distance, however, he pounced. Although he fortunately ended up with only a mouthful of Clarence's tail feathers and a severe scolding, such an incident could have had much more serious consequences! Apart from protection for the bird, you must consider your own property in the room. Although not as destructive with his beak as some parrot species, a cockatiel can do a fair bit of damage to things like papers, books, artificial and real plants. He can "try" your dinner and he can also knock objects off shelves or tables deliberately or accidentally. Therefore, if your bird is allowed regular access to the room, it is best to move any valuable items elsewhere.

have net curtains in front of the windows, so that the bird does not fly full pelt into the glass and severely injure himself. He should not be exposed to the dangers of open fires, hotplates or boiling food. Even if the fire is out, ensure that your cockatiel does not have access to the chimney; it is amazing where our mischievous little friend can get to if we are not careful. Other pets should be removed from the room; even the most trustworthy of cats and dogs will lick their

Training

Once your cockatiel is hand tame, he should also be repeating his first words. Assuming you have taught him his name first, the next thing is to try and teach him his address. This will be very useful should your bird accidentally escape at some time. Try to keep the address as simple as possible; just the number and name of your street should be adequate. Speech training can continue when he is in his cage or when he is sitting on your finger; continually repeat the word or phrase you wish him to learn in a clear manner and try and keep the tone of your voice similar for each individual word or phrase. At the same time, do not neglect previous words or phrases which he has already learned as he will forget them. Never try to teach him large new pieces of vocabulary until he has mastered the current ones, otherwise he will become confused and his sentences will become jumbled. Try and teach him complete words, phrases or sentences as individual units which cannot be easily confused with others. Once a cockatiel becomes accustomed to new words and sounds, he should

Food rewards are great motivating factors for a cockatiel in training. Millet sprays are great favorites, as are sunflower seeds and pieces of fruit.

learn quite rapidly; many cockatiels develop quite a repertoire in the first year of their lives. Some people use a tape recorder to teach their birds. The messages are repeated numerous times on the tape and then replayed over and over again near the bird. Although this is not as good as straight teaching, it does produce results and is useful for those who cannot spare the time.

A cockatiel can be trained to do little tricks as well as learn to talk. Rewards with tidbits are very useful to encourage him. Once he is finger tame you should have no trouble getting him to

The success of speech training depends greatly upon the talent of the individual bird.

24

come to your hand on command, especially if you repeat a word like "come," when you want him to sit on your finger. You can train him to jump from one finger to the other or from your finger to your shoulder or top of the head and, of course, he should be trained to return to his cage as soon as his playtime is over.

Birds which are reluctant to sit on your finger can be trained with a short piece of perch about 1.2cm (.5 in) in diameter. In the initial stages you can leave the training perch in his cage so that he becomes completely accustomed to it. To get the bird to return to his cage, you should get him onto your finger or training perch and slowly carry him to the cage door. After a time, he will understand your intentions and jump into the cage of his own account. It is not difficult to train a bird to return to his cage from anywhere in the room at the utterance of a simple command like "cage" or "house."

Toys for Cockatiels

A bird which spends long periods in his cage should

have various "toys" to occupy his mind and relieve boredom. Pet shops provide various safe toys which can be used, although cockatiels will play with almost anything. Small lengths of twig from non-poisonous trees can be given. These will allow the bird to exercise his beak as he strips off the bark, some of which he may also eat (which will do him no harm, provided the tree has not been treated with chemicals). The pieces of twig will be picked up, carried about, tossed in the air or pushed through the cage wire as the bird has his fun.

Pet shop toys include mirrors, bells and ladders. A mirror will occupy much of your bird's time and it should be given to him when he has to spend long periods of time alone in the cage. He will admire himself, talk to himself or attack his image; he may even fall in love with his own reflection, which is why the mirror should be removed when you are spending time with the bird, particularly during training sessions. Otherwise he will be so occupied with his reflection that he will

Some cockatiels will resort to biting during the initial taming sessions. Understand that the bird feels frightened, and patiently work toward making your pet feel at home. Never hit a bird for biting!

have no time for you!

A bell is also a useful toy; it may be made from metal or hard plastic and the bird will have great fun bashing the bell with his beak and delight in hearing its reaction. Ladders are made from hardwood or hard plastic and your cockatiel will spend hours dragging an object such as a piece of twig, a cotton reel or a coin up the ladder and dropping it on the cage floor, evidently enjoying the sound it makes. Chico, a pet cockatiel of the author's for many years, had a hard plastic casing from a ball point pen which he would play with for hours. He would drag it laboriously to the top of the cage, then drop it onto the floor before repeating the process time after time!

25

Foods and Feeding

Cockatiels are not difficult birds to feed and all of the basic nutrients will be included in a mixture of seeds, some greenfood or fruit, and a regular vitamin/mineral supplement. In the wild, the major part of a cockatiel's diet is the seeds of various grasses but they will supplement these with the seeds and buds of all manner of weeds, shrubs, and trees. They also enjoy the blossoms of certain native plants, including those of the many species of *Eucalyptus* found in the habitat. They have been observed digging at the roots of wild plants, much in the manner of but not as efficiently as the cockatoos with their more powerful bills. It is most probable that they take insect and other invertebrate food accidentally as they forage among the food plants and perhaps occasionally, deliberately. By this feeding strategy, the wild cockatiel is instinctively ensuring that it gets a balanced diet.

In captivity it would be almost impossible to provide cockatiels with the variety and type of foodstuffs they find in the wild, especially in countries other than Australia. We therefore have to provide a compromise which still contains a variety to ensure that our pets are

Peach-fronted conure and a cockatiel. Keep in mind that different birds will have different likes and dislikes.

The basic diet for a cockatiel is a blend of seeds and pellets. Fresh fruits and vegetables are also important nutritional supplements to your pet's diet. Remove uneaten fresh foods from the cage after a few hours.

receiving a balanced diet.

Seed: The staple part of the captive diet is seed, especially millet and canary seed, which will usually be obtained from pet shops and avicultural suppliers. Special cockatiel mixtures may also be available, these being composed of the dealer's idea of a balanced diet for the birds; but it is often safer, more fun and, incidentally, less expensive, to buy quantities of individual seeds and make up your own mixtures which can be varied, depending on the time of the year and whether your birds are breeding or molting. Like people, cockatiels can be very individualistic in their feeding habits and, while one specimen may be crazy about millet for example, another will prefer canary seed. In the following examples, ideas are given for two suitable staple diets; the first is richer in protein and fat than the second, and is suitable for offering during the breeding season and during the molt. During breeding, it will ensure that the parent birds are well equipped for the strenuous tasks of courting, mating, producing eggs, brooding and rearing the young (remembering that, in the wild, birds go to nest only during seasons in which food is bountiful), and that the young themselves receive adequate nutrients for growth. This diet is also suitable during the difficult molting period, to ensure a strong renewal of plumage. Outside the breeding season and the molt, things are much more relaxed, so the birds require a diet which will not lead to obesity.

Diet 1 (to be given during breeding and molting periods):

45% millet
(of various types)
30% canary seed
15% sunflower seed
5% oats
3% hemp
2% niger seed

Diet 2 (to be given during the resting period):

60% millet
(of various types)
24% canary seed
8% sunflower seed
3% oats
3% hemp
2% niger seed

Note: Sunflower seed and hemp should not be given in greater percentages than those stated above. Both of these seeds are very high in oil (fat) content and, although the birds may be crazy about them, excessive quantities will lead to obesity and poor breeding results.

Various kinds of bird seeds are supplied in paper or plastic bags. If one has a large number of birds, it may be more economical to buy seeds in larger bulk than one would for a single pet or a couple of breeding pairs. With larger quantities of seed, however, efficient means of storing it must be considered. It should be kept in a dry, ventilated room (many aviculturists include special storage space for seed in their bird rooms or incorporate them in the shelter part of outside aviaries) and preferably transferred from the delivery sacks into metal bins with good fitting lids. This will discourage rodents and invertebrate pests from eating and tainting the seed and keep it dry. Special galvanized metal seed bins are supplied by dealers in avicultural goods but galvanized metal trash cans are just as effective and probably cheaper. For smaller quantities of seeds, aluminum or stainless steel dry-food canisters may be used.

The seed may be fed to the birds in stainless steel, aluminum, porcelain, or glass containers or hoppers (many plastic accessories are available but these tend to weather quickly and are easily broken; there is also the danger of birds gnawing at the plastic and ingesting it). Self-filling hoppers are useful as a ration of seed for a few days at a time can be supplied. However, one should ensure that the empty seed husks are regularly removed from the feeding surfaces. This is done by simply stirring the surface of the seed and gently blowing the husks away. Most birds shell the seeds before swallowing the kernel and, more often than not, the empty husks fall back into the food container, eventually covering the uneaten seed entirely. It is not unknown for birds to have starved when having an almost full seed hopper, just because their owner did not have the presence of mind to remove the husks. It would be an economical proposition to invest in a small winnower, especially where larger quantities of seed are concerned. Such a winnower, obtainable from avicultural suppliers, can be regularly used to recycle uneaten seed from the dishes and hoppers. Open seed containers should also be emptied and cleaned out at regular intervals. They should never be placed below perches, where they would quickly become soiled with bird droppings. The most suitable spot in the aviary is on a feeding platform, under the covered part, to prevent rain wetting it.

Soaked Seed: An excellent way of giving your birds a variation in the diet and, at the same time, improving the nutritional value of it, is to provide seed which has been soaked in water. By immersing seed in water and leaving it to soak for not more than 24 hours (leaving it longer than this will cause it to ferment, producing alcohol and other substances which could be dangerous to the health of your birds), the process of germination will commence, causing chemical changes within. Protein levels will

"It is not unknown for birds to have starved when having an almost full seed hopper, just because their owner did not have the presence of mind to remove the husks."

29

increase and the contents of the seed will become more easily digestible. During the breeding season in particular, soaked seed is of excellent value, especially during the rearing of the nestlings; the partially digested seed passed to them by the parents will be in a more acceptable and nutritious form. Soaked seed can also be used as a tonic for birds suffering from stress (particularly after a change of accommodation), during treatment or recovery from a disease. It should not replace the ordinary dry seed, but can be offered at regular intervals throughout the year (say once per week) and daily during the breeding season.

Most kinds of bird seed are suitable for soaking and you may desire to soak a made-up mixture or prepare individual types to be given on a basis of rotation. Only small amounts of seed (enough for one day) should be prepared at a time as such mixtures tend to sour very quickly (particularly in warmer weather) and could thus cause stomach upsets. The required amount of seed is placed in a suitable container and a quantity of cold, or very slightly lukewarm water is poured over it until the grains are freely floating. After stirring it about to ensure that all individual grains are wet, the container should be placed in a warm spot (in the airing cupboard for example) and left for 24 hours. It should then be drained through a fine meshed sieve and rinsed thoroughly with clean, cold water. The seed can then be partially dried by tipping it out onto, and dabbing it with, an absorbent towel. The soaked seed should be served to the birds in a clean, shallow dish; any seed which is uneaten by the end of the day should be removed and discarded.

Millet Sprays: The natural ears from the living millet plant are normally referred to by aviculturists as millet sprays. Quantities of the sprays are dried out without being thrashed for the avicultural trade. By supplying a certain amount of the birds' diet on sprays a more natural pattern of feeding will be accomplished. Captive birds seem to delight in removing the seeds from the sprays, much in the manner as they would in the wild, even though it means more work than simply picking up seeds from the feeding dish. Millet sprays should therefore be given conservatively as there is a danger that the winnowed seed (and the variety) will be ignored. Perhaps one millet spray per pair of birds twice per week can be considered sufficient. Millet sprays may also be soaked and prepared in the same way as ordinary seed. The sprays can be tied or clipped to the cage or aviary wire so that the birds derive exercise in clambering about to remove the seeds.

Greenfood and Fruit: It is important that cockatiels are given a regular supply and variety of greenfood and fruit in order to supplement their staple diet of seeds. Fresh greenfood and fruit contain a number of vitamins in greater quantity than found in the seeds and birds will enjoy these additions to the diet. That old standby greenfood, lettuce, is usually eagerly accepted but not of great nutritional value. Spinach is more nutritious and is usually taken eagerly; it may be grown in the

Seeding grasses in season are eagerly accepted and they are highly nutritious. Other weeds such as dandelion, groundsel, shepherds purse, chickweed, plantains, and so on, all have a value if given in small quantities. Certain weeds of course may not be available in some countries and will be replaced by others. If unsure about the food value of certain weeds, consult other aviculturists or even keepers of chickens and rabbits to see what wild foods are given to their livestock.

When collecting wild greenfood, ensure that no poisonous plants are hidden in the bundle. It is best to avoid collecting near road verges where plants may be polluted by vehicle fumes or the droppings of domestic animals. Also, never use anything which you suspect has been treated with insecticides, herbicides or artificial fertilizers; some of these chemicals could be highly dangerous to the health of your birds. Bundles of greenfood can be secured with a piece of sisal string high up on the wire of the cage or aviary and the birds

Cuttlefish bone (or cuttlebone), the internal shell of the cuttlefish, is an excellent source of calcium for cage birds.

garden for most of the year. Many other items from the vegetable garden, including small pieces of carrot, swede or turnip, cabbage, peas (and pods), runner beans, and others may be taken. Not all birds will take everything you offer, but there is no harm in experimenting.

will derive some exercise from pulling pieces off. Twigs from fruit and other non-poisonous trees, complete with buds and leaves, can also be given and the birds will have fun stripping off the bark and eating the buds and leaves.

Most cockatiels enjoy nibbling at fruit and a regular piece of apple, pear, plum, banana, or orange may be given. The best way to give fruit is to impale a piece on a spike that has been driven through one of the perches. Half an orange can be given in this way and most cockatiels will enjoy nibbling at it. Smaller fruits such as grapes, raspberries, blackberries, gooseberries, and currants may also be offered in small quantities. Greenfood and fruit should be given regularly and sparingly but, at the first signs of diarrhea in your stock, revert immediately to a dry-food only regimen until the problem has been alleviated.

Tidbits: Many keepers of cockatiels, particularly those with a pet bird, delight in giving them tidbits. Although it is perfectly all right to do this, one should

act with restraint as birds get into the habit of preferring items of food which are not best for them in too large quantities. Most cockatiels love all forms of breakfast cereals and a friend of the author's had a bird which, when let out of his cage, made immediately for the cornflakes box, going in head first! All kinds of cake may be offered in small quantities and wholemeal bread may also be given (avoid white bread unless it has first been allowed to go stale).

One treat which the birds

A pair of cockatiels with millet spray, a favorite of many cage birds. In fact, millet spray is so popular among parrots that many experts believe it should be given only as a treat, as its presence causes birds to ignore their staple food.

will enjoy very much can be made up as follows: dissolve one teaspoonful of honey in five teaspoonsful of warm milk, then mix with enough plain sponge cake to form a semi-runny paste. This can be given in a small dish. It is a very nutritious mixture and can be offered to sick birds as a tonic or can be given two or three times a week to breeding birds. For normal, fit birds outside the breeding season, it should not be given more than once per week.

Grit and Cuttlefish Bone: The digestive system of any bird demands that it has grit in its gizzard. The bird swallows small stones, pieces of gravel and other insoluble materials and these are used for grinding the food into a fluid mass before it passes on through the system. The grit itself remains in the gizzard. Birds also derive valuable trace elements from grit as it is gradually worn down by the action of the muscular gizzard walls. A bird with no access to grit will be unable to digest its food properly and will soon become anemic. Grit, consisting of a mixture of crushed stones,

washed, crushed seashells, and pieces of cuttlefish bone, may be obtained from your avicultural suppliers. Bird sand, supplied for use on the floors of cages, may also contain a proportion of grit. Grit can best be served in special dishes or dispensers separate from the food, so that you can easily monitor how much is being taken. If birds in outdoor aviaries do not seem to be taking much grit from your supply, do not worry; they will be taking items from the flight floor in preference. There is little you can do to stop this, and as long as they are getting grit in some form or other it does not matter. However, to be on the safe side, extra grit should always be available.

One of the most important minerals in the diet is calcium, which is essential for the forming of strong egg shells, and the bones in growing chicks; it is also of importance in feather growth. Probably the most convenient way of supplying additional calcium to cage and aviary birds, and one which they seem to enjoy, is to offer them cuttlefish bone. This is the internal skeleton of the squid-like cuttlefish and is rich in calcium salts as well as a small quantity of other trace elements. Prepared cuttlefish bones can be purchased from your supplier and they may be fitted with a bulldog clip to the cage or aviary wire. The birds will then be able to break off pieces as they require them. Chewing at cuttlefish bone will also help the birds keep their beaks in trim. Cuttlefish bones may be found on the seashore, but these should first be treated to remove dirt and sea-salt before giving them to the birds. It is best to soak them in running water for 48 hours, before drying them out (in the sun) and using them. Eggshells are also rich in calcium and those of domestic chickens (after you have eaten the contents) can be saved, then baked in the oven until brittle (but not burnt) before being crushed and added to the birds' grit.

Other Supplements and Tonics: Many proprietary brands of vitamin and mineral supplements are available from avicultural suppliers. These vary in quality and effect and it is best to select only well-known brands or those with a proven track record. Vitamin/mineral tonics can be particularly useful during times of breeding and molting, when the birds' health is under pressure. Supplements may be available in fluid form for adding to drinking water; in powder form, for adding to the food, or in block form for clipping to the cage wire. Use such supplements according to the manufacturer's instructions

Feather plucking may be caused by a vitamin deficiency. A well-balanced diet and the proper use of vitamin/mineral supplements should keep your pet happy and healthy.

35

and never be tempted to give too much; overdoses of certain vitamins or minerals can be more dangerous than not supplying any at all.

Cockatiels may be occasionally observed eating their own droppings or those of other birds. To our human minds, this may seem like a disgusting habit but, in the wild, many animals and birds do this and there is a logical explanation. Certain vitamins of the B complex, particularly B_2 (riboflavin) and B_{12} (cyanocobalamine), are actually manufactured in the gut of the living animal during digestion. By eating the droppings, birds are instinctively ensuring an adequate supply of these vitamins. Unfortunately, certain diseases are also transmitted through droppings, so the habit should be discouraged as far as possible by supplying vitamin/mineral supplements and keeping food containers clear of perches.

Water: Although water is not usually classed as part of the diet (in its pure form it contains no nutrients) it is a commodity which is essential to life. Indeed, water forms at least 90% of all living organisms. Birds taking regular quantities of food with a high water content (greenfood, fruit, etc.) will not drink as much as birds taking mainly seed. However, fresh water must be available at all times. In a cage, the water can be given in a special dish or water fountain. Whatever is used, the container must be cleaned daily and replenished with fresh water; tap water is quite adequate. In aviaries, the water can be supplied in a small pond. This need be nothing more than a large, shallow dish, with water in it to not more than 2.5cm (1 in) deep. If the edges of the dish are deeper than this, holes should be drilled to let the excess water out and maintain the depth should it fill with rain; otherwise there might be the risk of birds drowning, particularly fledglings. The birds may use the dish for bathing as well as drinking but it is pointless having a separate drinking vessel as the birds will not distinguish between the two.

If you want a better looking pond in the outdoor flight, you can construct one from concrete. Prepare a small quantity of concrete (say 1 shovel of cement to 2 shovels of sand and three of pea shingle) and mix to a workable consistency with water. The concrete is placed on top of a waterproof polyethylene sheet (of the type used by builders for dampproofing) in a slight hollow in the aviary floor and shaped, using a trowel, to form a shallow pond. For added strength, some galvanized mesh can be placed inside the concrete. It should be smoothed over with a soft brush before it sets, to make it easier to clean. To make it more natural looking you may like to include a few rocks in the border, but ensure that there is a run-off so that the water cannot get too deep if it rains. The birds should obviously have no access to the concrete until it is thoroughly set and, if they are already in residence, it can be protected with a piece of aviary wire. If the pond is constructed in very hot weather, it should be covered with a piece of damp sacking while it is setting, so that it does not crack from drying out too

Natural branch perches are great for chewing and they provide valuable trace elements.

quickly. Once set, the pond should be filled with water and allowed to stand for 24 hours before scrubbing the surface thoroughly to remove lime deposits. The pond is now ready for use; it should be swept out daily with a bast broom and replenished with fresh water and, at regular intervals, the surfaces should be scrubbed with a mild solution of bleach. Needless to say, no water bath should be situated under a perch or other place where it could quickly become fouled with droppings.

37

Breeding Cockatiels

To many birdkeepers, the most satisfying aspect of the hobby is to get their charges to breed. Many keepers of a single pet cockatiel have developed into breeders at a later date; indeed, some of the top breeders originally had their appetites whetted by keeping a single pet bird. The pet bird which has become one of the family does not, however, always make a good breeder; it will probably think it is a human being and have no interest in a cockatiel mate, other than as an item of annoyance! It is therefore recommended that such a bird remains a pet and that fresh stock be acquired if you intend to breed cockatiels.

Foundation Stock

Cockatiels are one of the few parrot-like birds which can be bred safely on the colony system. In other words, you can keep as many pairs in the same aviary as space (or expense) permits, without danger of serious injury resulting from rivalry between males. Colony breeding is an interesting method, as it allows the birds to choose their own mates and they can behave in the hierarchical manner which would prevail in the wild. Youngsters produced in colony breeding should be of good average quality, but will rarely be of a standard suitable for exhibition. If you want to produce exhibition-standard offspring, then it will be necessary to carry out selective breeding by pairing up good quality birds and keeping them in separate breeding accommodations.

The type of foundation stock you acquire will therefore depend on which type of breeding you intend to carry out. In the author's opinion, all newcomers to cockatiel breeding should initially buy cheaper stock, say three pairs, and attempt colony breeding to gain

Opposite: Only cockatiels in perfect health and great physical condition should be bred. Never breed a sick cockatiel!

Pied cockatiels are bred for clear, sharp markings. Perfecting a color strain can be quite a challenge.

valuable general breeding experience before embarking on more ambitious projects. It is worth pointing out here that prize-winning birds or the offspring therefrom do not necessarily make the best pets; in fact mongrels are frequently more intelligent and have greater learning powers than the most expensive of champions.

Suitable birds may be obtained from pet shops, dealers or breeders and should be selected carefully, ensuring that only birds in the best of health are purchased. If, at a later date, you wish to start breeding exhibition stock, you must obtain your foundation pair (more than a single pair is usually financially out of the question) from a breeder with a proven exhibition record and the birds should preferably be offspring or close relatives of previous prize winners.

When to Breed

Cockatiels may attempt to breed at any time of the year. If you are keeping them in indoor breeding cages or aviaries, this does not matter so much, but if the birds are in outdoor aviaries, they should be denied the opportunity to breed during the cold parts of the year (this is done by simply not giving them a nest box). Indoor breeding ensures that the birds are protected from the weather, but generations of birds bred in this way may decrease in size, lose condition and appear anemic. There is no doubt that healthy outdoor living is beneficial to cockatiels and the quality of their offspring. One compromise method is to keep the birds in an outdoor aviary outside the breeding season and to introduce them into an indoor breeding cage when you are ready to breed them. If a number of birds are kept together in the outdoor aviary, however, you must ensure that bonded pairs remain together; cockatiels normally pair up for life and separation may set back breeding prospects.

In the northern hemisphere, nestboxes should be put out at around the middle of April or when all dangers of severe frosts have abated. Cockatiels may rear several clutches a year, but any more than three should be avoided as the parents will become exhausted and start losing condition. After the third clutch leaves the nest, the nest box should be removed immediately. In any case, outside breeding should be stopped by the middle of September.

Nest Boxes

Whether breeding in cages or aviaries indoors or in outdoor aviaries, good quality nestboxes are

Nine-day-old cockatiel chick. Note how the feathers are starting to grow in.

essential. In the wild, cockatiels usually nest in hollowed out tree stumps and branches. If the cavity is too small the birds will make it larger by chewing at the lining. There is tremendous competition for suitable nest sites and birds will select cavities between 1 and 8m (3-25 ft) from the ground. Although natural log nestboxes may be used for captive breeding, it is more convenient to manufacture or purchase compromise boxes made from timber.

The best type of timber to use is 2cm (0.75 in) thick planking; the harder the wood is, the better. The minimum internal measurements for a nest box should be 37.5cm high x 25cm x 25cm (15 x 10 x 10 in). Although the author prefers the vertical type of box, good results may also be obtained with horizontal boxes, providing the nest chamber is well away from the entrance hole. The entrance hole can be about 7.5cm (3 in) in diameter, just wide enough for the birds to enter, and should be just below the roof of a vertical box, or at one end of a horizontal one. There should be a short perch, firmly affixed just below the entrance hole, so that the birds have easy access. Some breeders like to provide a nest hollow, made from a separate piece of timber, which may be obtained from avicultural suppliers. It should fit the base of the nest box exactly, leaving no gaps into which eggs could accidentally fall.

The nest box should have a hinged inspection door, preferably in the lower front, so that one can easily examine the clutch and the nestlings when the parent birds are absent. A low safety panel should be placed at the bottom of the door, to prevent eggs or nestlings from accidentally falling out when it is opened. The box should have a waterproof sloping roof with a slight overhang. The boxes are best fixed in the flight as high up as possible, but all at the same height for the colony system, to prevent squabbling for the highest sites. There should be extra nestboxes for the birds so that they have a choice; for each two pairs of birds, provide three boxes. Of course, a single pair of birds will usually make do with any box you give them. A thin layer (about 1 cm or ⅜ in) of rotting wood (from non-poisonous trees), damp

sawdust or peat may be placed in the base of the box. This will ensure humidity for the developing eggs. Some breeders like to have a double bottom in the box so that a tray of water can be placed between the two floors and help keep humid conditions. In the wild, birds often wet their feathers by bathing before they take their turn at brooding. Some captive birds may also exhibit this behavior.

Breeding Behavior

The courtship behavior of cockatiels is not as spectacular as some birds

A trio of cockatiel chicks inside the nestbox. Your pet shop will provide several types of shavings to use as litter.

43

but nonetheless interesting, even amusing to watch. The male will display to the female (who will initially appear to take no notice) by running up and down the perch, letting out his shrill whistle and song and occasionally spreading his wing and tail feathers. He will raise and lower his crest and sometimes hang upside down on the perch. Both sexes will show interest in the chosen nest box and will, at first, peer into the entrance in a comical manner, examining the inside with great detail, but not entering at first (perhaps ensuring that there is nobody already in there). Eventually the cock will sidle up to the hen and mount her. If she is receptive, she will stay put and allow him to maneuver his vent in apposition to hers for copulation to take place. It is important that perches be firmly fixed; insecure perches can lead to abortive matings!

The average number of eggs in a clutch is five, but may be as low as one or as high as eight. It is best to allow the birds to incubate no more than five eggs. On the colony system, excess eggs in one nest can be shared out with birds with fewer eggs, so that each pair has a maximum of four or five chicks to rear. Larger clutches can result in the parents being unable to cope with the feeding and the subsequent loss of some or all of the chicks. The eggs are white, about 2.5cm (1 in) in length and 2cm (0.75 in) in width. They are laid every other day and serious incubation begins after the second or third egg. The period of incubation is 19-21 days. The later laid eggs will of course hatch a day or two later than the earlier ones but this generally has no serious consequences.

Both cock and hen share in the incubation of the eggs and the brooding of the chicks; the male will enter the box in the morning and stay until late afternoon, when he is relieved by the female who stays in the nest overnight. If you want to inspect the nest, this should be done at brood change over time so that there is minimum disturbance. Young cockatiels will express their displeasure at being inspected by hissing and swaying their bodies

44

from side to side. Inspections should not be carried out too often; you can usually tell if there is something wrong by the behavior of the birds (for example, the pair may be absent from the nest for unusually long periods or abandon the nest altogether). Undue disturbance by cats, dogs, vermin, wild animals, people, and yourself are factors which en-courage birds to abandon their broods, so great care needs to be taken at this time. If the birds should abandon the nest, the eggs or chicks may be fostered out to a more reliable pair of birds.

In extreme cases (loss of one or both parents, or total abandonment), the chicks may be hand-reared. This is a difficult task requiring much patience. The chick(s) should be placed in a cardboard box on a few wood shavings and kept in a warm place (around 28°C or 82°F). A good rearing food is a thin oatmeal porridge prepared with a 50/50 mixture of lukewarm milk and water. Tinned or bottled baby food (of the vegetable and cereal kind) may also be used. The food is given by means of a syringe, an eye dropper or a small spoon. As the birds grow, they can be fed on more substantial food, including soaked seed and green food which is mixed

Young lutino cockatiel with two eggs. You can tell that this bird is a lutino by its pink eyes.

45

Left: Cockatiel embryo. *Right:* Nine-day-old chick.

Six-day-old chick.

Ten-day-old chick.

Two-week-old (14 days) chick.

46

with a little water and ground up by pestle and mortar. Pick up the bird and feed as described for sick birds. The younger the birds, the thinner the food and the more frequent the feeding. You may have to feed them up to ten times a day, ensuring the crop is full after each session. You stand a 50/50 chance of successfully rearing young chicks but as they grow, they will accept food more readily and will soon become tame. In fact, hand-reared birds make the best pets. In most cases, however, you should have no problems, especially if you use breeding pairs over nine months old. Birds younger than this may breed but their behavior can be erratic and unreliable, and there is a danger of egg-binding in the hen. To be on the safe side, most successful breeders use birds not less than one year old. On hatching, the chicks are covered in a yellow down and within 20 days the feather quills will be in an advanced stage of development. Both parents will feed the young from crop-milk, partially digested and liquefied food from the parent crop. It is most important to the health of the youngsters that the adults receive a wide variety of food during this time.

At 35 days they will be almost fully feathered and ready to leave the nest. They will be flying in a very short time and the parents will continue to feed them for about 14 days. It is best to remove them to separate accommodation as soon as they are feeding themselves as the parents may want to start on a second clutch.

Ringing or Banding

The serious cockatiel breeder will want to keep records. It is wise to have a breeding record book or a card index system with a page or a card for each bird. The owner of a home computer will find it invaluable for keeping readily accessible records. To keep a check on individual birds, they should have leg bands. Split rings

Fifteen-day-old chick.

Seventeen-day-old chick.

Twenty-day-old chick.

Twenty-two–day-old chick.

made of hard, colored plastic are useful for distinguishing adult pairs being kept on the colony system. These are simply applied around the leg using a special banding tool. Once you are breeding birds on a regular basis, the chicks can be closed-ringed, this being done when they are seven to ten days old. Numbered aluminum rings for cockatiels may be purchased from your avicultural supplier. The rings are pushed over the bird's foot; the front two toes first and then the rear two toes are held along the leg so that the ring can be slid onto the leg. It may help to apply a little thick petroleum jelly to the foot, to stick the toes together and provide lubrication (this should be wiped off afterwards). The bird will grow and once in position the ring will stay on permanently. By having a numbered ring, you can keep individual records of breeding performance, behavior, sicknesses or other relevant information which may be useful for advancement of the science. At some stage, you may want to write an article on particular experiences for the benefit of other aviculturists. For this, your records will be invaluable.

Breeding Problems

If the birds are kept in hygienic conditions and given all the care that is described in this book, your breeding season should be relatively problem-free. The main problems which occur occasionally include French molt and egg-binding. This latter condition is potentially fatal and an afflicted hen must be treated without delay. An egg becomes lodged in the ovary of the bird and she will soon take on a sorry appearance, sitting and moping, with her feathers fluffed out. If a hen appears sick in the early stages of breeding, egg-binding must be the first thing to suspect. There are several possible causes for this condition, most of which are preventable. They include shortage of calcium, chilling and immaturity of the bird concerned (that is why it is recommended that birds should be at least nine months—preferably one year old—before being allowed to breed). In the case of a

"If the birds are kept in hygienic conditions and given all the care that is described in this book, your breeding season should be relatively problem-free."

48

Sometimes cockatiel mates are simply not compatible. If you notice evidence of undue squabbling among the birds, separate them and try again. If they still don't get along, pair them with other birds.

calcium deficiency, the eggs may have a soft, rubbery shell and will not pass easily through the oviduct. An egg-bound hen should be placed in a warm environment (hospital cage) and maintained at a temperature of about 30°C (86°F). In many cases, this heat treatment alone is enough to ensure that the egg is successfully passed. In stubborn cases a veterinarian should be consulted as soon as possible; an injection of calcium borogluconate may help relieve the disorder. Birds which have suffered from egg-binding should not be used again for breeding for at least 12 months.

Failure of eggs to hatch is a fairly common occurrence and can be caused by their being infertile (ensure that you have a true pair and not two hens or two cocks!) due to the birds being immature or for various technical reasons. In some cases one or more eggs in a clutch will be infertile, while the others will hatch normally. You can

49

Never breed an immature cockatiel. Not only will the offspring from such a bird be inferior, but the bird's health may be affected as well.

Opposite: Don't breed a cockatiel with a nasty temper, as this trait might be passed on to its young.

A pair of lutino cockatiels.

which have been scared from the nest), or poor humidity in the nest box. Poor humidity will cause the eggs to lose moisture and the embryos will desiccate and die. Breeding birds should always have access to a bath so that they can wet their feathers and carry moisture back to the nest. Poor humidity problems are unlikely with birds being bred outdoors but those indoors, particularly in cages, should be kept under observation. Birds which refuse to bathe should be regularly sprayed with a fine mist spray of warm water.

tell if eggs are fertile after they have been brooded for four or five days by *candling* them. Cut a small hole in a piece of thick cardboard, just large enough to take an egg, and hold the egg in the hole in front of a strong light. A fertile egg will show a dark embryo shadow, will be pink in color and blood vessels may be visible; an infertile or *clear* egg will have no shadow and will appear yellowish.

Sometimes, chicks may die in the shell; this can also be caused by several things including dietary deficiency in the hen, irregular brooding (by immature or nervous birds or by birds

Cockatiel Varieties

"Being virtually domesticated and easy to breed, cockatiels are already available in a fairly wide range of color varieties. These are really mutations which would not survive for long in the wild, but are nurtured in captivity for their esthetic attraction."

Being virtually domesticated and easy to breed, cockatiels are already available in a fairly wide range of color varieties. These are really mutations which would not survive for long in the wild, but are nurtured in captivity for their esthetic attraction. A mutation is a diversion from the normal and tiny mutations are occurring all the time in successive generations of animals. Those mutations which are not favorable to continued existence quickly disappear (for example, an albino or lutino cockatiel in the wild would be more easily spotted by a predator), while favorable mutations will gradually modify stock over periods of time. This is another form of evolution by natural selection.

Great excitement occurs among aviculturists when a new color mutation appears in captive stock. In some cases, initial mutations are extremely valuable and fetch very high prices from breeders. The first owner of a white cockatiel for example, would have been sitting on a gold mine. However, as these mutations are nurtured and selectively bred to produce more of the same kind, the prices gradually come down to more reasonable levels.

The normal wild cockatiel has been fully described and, in its natural range there is very little color variation. In some areas birds may be darker or lighter, or their color patches may differ slightly, but in general, each wild cockatiel is colored similarly to the next. This color and pattern is the one most ideally suited to the cockatiel in its habitat at the present time and probably provides good camouflage, particularly when the birds are perched on dead limbs. The following text describes the best known cockatiel color mutations and is followed by a discussion on color breeding.

The Lutino

This is probably the most popular color mutation and it first appeared in Florida, U.S.A. during 1958. Early examples of the bird were referred to as moonbeams after the late Mrs. E. L. Moon who was largely responsible for the proliferation of the variety. The lutino bird has lost all of the dark pigment in its plumage and appears to be white, washed with yellow. The head remains bright yellow and the orange cheek patches, though somewhat lighter than in the normal bird, are plainly evident. Cocks and hens are very similar, but it is easy to distinguish adults as the barring in the tail of the hen occurs in yellow, this being absent in the cock. The eyes are dark red, the legs and feet pink, the cere pink and the beak buff.

The Albino

This has gone a stage further than the lutino and has lost the yellow wash pigment in its plumage as well as the dark although it still has a yellow head and

Lutino cockatiel. This color variety has become increasingly popular over the past few years.

orange cheek patches. The bird is otherwise pure white with red eyes. Its legs, feet, cere, and beak are pink. It is difficult to distinguish the sexes, though ghost markings of the bars in the adult hen's tail may be apparent.

The Pied or Harlequin

The pied mutation was the first major one to appear in captivity but its origins are still obscure. However, it was almost certain to have appeared in the U.S.A. prior to 1950 and stock from there was used to found European strains. In pied cockatiels, the dark pigment has only

53

Pearled or pearl cockatiel. As breeders continue to perfect this variety, more and more color-phase pearls will be seen.

transferring the normal gray coloration to a deep rich fawn. The yellow and orange head markings may also be somewhat lighter than in the normal. The feet and legs are deep fleshy pink and the beak horny gray. The sexes may be distinguished in the same way as with the normal gray. Some very pale fawns are referred to as Creme, especially in continental Europe.

Pearled or Lace

The pearled cockatiel has developed markings similar to those seen in the opaline budgerigar. Large areas of plumage, especially on the upper parts, have lost pigment in the center of the individual feathers but a gray border has remained, giving a two-toned effect. The central patch of each feather is grayish-white, while the border remains normal gray. The other colors are similar to those of the normal and it is relatively easy to distinguish the sexes of adults. This variety was first seen in West Germany in the late 1960's and appeared in Belgium a little later. It is now a very popular variety. Birds with more

partly been lost, leaving patches of white in the normal plumage. These white patches vary considerably in size and shape and may appear on any part of the body. If the tail is affected, it becomes difficult to determine the sex, even in adults. Pieds have been interbred with other color mutations to produce some startling color variants.

Fawn, Cinnamon or Isabelle

This variety was first bred in Belgium during the early 1960's. The dark pigment (or melanin) has become diluted, yellow wash in the feathers may sometimes be referred to as golden-laced pearls as opposed to the usual type, which may be called silver-laced pearls.

Silver

This variety is similarly marked to the normal, but the gray plumage is replaced by silvery gray. The normal sex differences apply. The silver first appeared in Belgium in the late 1950's; then it seems to have been lost for a period of about ten years before it reappeared. The eyes are red and initial stock seems to have been afflicted with problems of semi-blindness and poor fertility. Selective breeding has now largely overcome these problems and the variety appears to be becoming more popular.

White-faced

This is a relatively new mutation, in which the yellow and orange pigment has been lost. Birds are marked as normals but the yellow areas are replaced with white. It is easy to distinguish the sexes of the adult by the barring in the hen's tail. It was thought to have first appeared in Holland in 1964 but it remained scarce until the late 70's when it re-appeared in Germany. It is now being bred in reasonable numbers.

Composite Variants

In addition to the main mutant colors, birds of composite coloring are frequently seen. These include such delights as pied fawn, pied pearled, pearled fawn, and pied pearled fawn. As experimentation in color breeding progresses it is likely that further mutants and composite variants are produced. At present, most color mutations seem to be based on a loss or reduction of melanin (dark pigment) but it is quite possible that an increase in the pigment will produce an almost black individual in the future. It is also possible that green pigment is present in the normal cockatiel, and this has been demonstrated by the appearance of the occasional olive-green. However, no strains seem to have become firmly established in this color, although ongoing experimentation is sure to produce some startling results in the future.

"In addition to the main mutant colors, birds of composite coloring are frequently seen . . . As experimentation in color breeding progresses it is likely that further mutants and composite variants are produced."

Health and Hygiene

Health is a difficult word to describe. In the dictionary at hand, it is defined as wholeness or soundness, especially of the body; general state of the body. The best way to discuss health, however, is to understand that there is good health and bad health. If we are serious about our pet birds, we obviously want them to remain in good health at all times, and the way to accomplish this is to ensure that our practices of hygiene are adequate. Hygiene is the science of promoting good health and preventing disease; thus, if our hygiene is bad, it will lead to bad health of one form or another. Remember that you can have good health and you can have bad health; there is no in-between state of health.

When one keeps groups of birds (or any animals for that matter) in close confinement, good hygienic practices are essential.

Infectious disease will quickly spread from one bird to the next unless strict precautions are taken. Hygiene sometimes sounds more complicated than it really is but all it takes to keep your birds in the best of health is thoughtful and thorough husbandry. Cockatiels provided with the correct nourishment, kept in clean, dry, damp-proof and vermin-free quarters and kept free of stress should live to a ripe old age of 20 years or more.

Choosing Stock

Perhaps the primary rule of hygiene in aviculture is to ensure that healthy stock is acquired in the first instance. Stock should be purchased only from approved dealers and breeders. Dubious or unclean premises should be avoided and it is always best to collect your birds personally, even if there is some kind of guarantee of live arrival. Select specimens which are clean, bright-eyed and full-colored with tight, neat plumage. Birds with ruffled feathers, bald patches or which are moping in some corner showing little interest in their surroundings should not be purchased. A healthy bird is alert, nervous, and ready to make its escape should you try to catch it. If possible, handle the birds before purchase and examine them closely. It may be necessary to wear stout gloves when handling untamed birds as they are capable of giving a painful nip with their beaks. Birds are usually caught up in aviaries in a soft-rimmed net, then transferred to the hand. If in a small cage, the bird can be caught straight into the hand. Hold it gently but firmly with its back in the palm of the hand, gripping the whole body around the wings and restraining the head with two fingers around the neck. This will allow you to examine the vent, which should be clean and free of any wetness or encrustations. With the other hand, gently unfold the wings, one at a time, and examine for injuries or deformities. Look

The best "cure" for cockatiel disease is prevention. Proper hygiene will go a long way toward keeping your pet healthy and long-lived.

at the eyes, nostrils, and mouth for signs of discharges and blow gently into the feathers to look for parasites or skin blemishes. After ascertaining that your purchase is as healthy as it can be, it may be packed into a travelling box and transported home as quickly as possible. Most bird dealers will supply specially made little cardboard transport boxes which hold just one bird. Do not be tempted to open the box and have another look at the bird while you are in transit; many new purchases have been lost in this way!

Quarantine

It is important that all new acquisitions are given a period of quarantine before being introduced to existing stock. If you are buying your first pair of birds, or a single pet, special quarantine quarters are unnecessary of course, but if you have existing stock, the new birds must be kept separately, preferably in a cage in a different room, for a period of at least 14 days. This is in addition to any statutory quarantine which the dealer may have been obliged to carry out and is a period of isolation, allowing one to watch for any signs of disease, which may have been undetectable at the time of purchase, but which may show symptoms later. If any signs of disease occur during the quarantine period, treatment should be carried out and the sick bird kept well away from other stock until completely cured. Should no sign of sickness occur during the quarantine period then it is reasonably safe to introduce the bird to existing stock.

Diseases and Treatment

As discussed above,

"If any signs of disease occur during the quarantine period, treatment should be carried out and the sick bird kept well away from other stock until completely cured."

cockatiels kept in hygienic conditions should remain ailment-free. However, there is a variety of diseases to which they are susceptible and it is wise to know what to do should a bird suddenly fall ill. A sick bird will sit moping in a corner or at the end of a perch, with its feathers fluffed out, often with its head tucked under its wing. It will lose its appetite and consequently, its weight and condition will rapidly deteriorate. A bird which has been off its food for a few days through sickness will show a characteristic hollowing of the breast on either side of the sternum (breastbone). Such symptoms are characteristic of many diseases, some of which may be diagnosed by additional symptoms. If you are unsure about the nature of the disease in question and do not know how to treat it, a veterinarian should be consulted. Some veterinarians specialize in bird diseases, and your regular vet will consult with an expert or put you in touch with one.

As soon as a sick bird is discovered it should be

isolated from other stock and put in a warm, dry, draft-proof place, preferably in the shade. Many sick birds will respond to quiet rest and heat treatment. Owners of several birds will find it useful to have a special hospital cage. Such a cage has a glass front to prevent drafts and heat loss (the glass is slid in position over the wire front in special grooves), is heated from the base (often by a simple light bulb under a false floor), and the temperature can be adjusted with a thermostat to stay at a range of levels. The sick bird is placed in the cage and the temperature maintained at about 32°C. Sick birds will often go off their food, and more often than not it is starvation that causes their death rather than the disease itself. The bird's favorite food should be placed within easy reach of the perch and, of course, fresh water should be available at all times. The bird can be encouraged to feed by offering it additional tidbits, but if this fails it should be hand fed to help it maintain its energy sources. A good energy producing and disease-fighting food can be made by mixing a teaspoon of honey or golden syrup into a cup of hot milk; then add an egg yolk and a tiny pinch of salt. Mix thoroughly and allow to cool to lukewarm; then it can be fed to the bird drop by drop. Pick the bird up in the hand (as described earlier) and, with the thumb and forefinger of the same hand, the beak can be gently forced open. Using a syringe or eye dropper (which can be obtained from a drug store) the food is dropped into the gullet. Alternatively, the fluid may be dribbled into the bird's throat from a teaspoon. Medicines prescribed by a veterinarian may be administered in a similar manner.

Wounds and Injuries

These are caused by such things as fighting (rare in cockatiels) or by flying into glass or cage wire after a panic. Injured birds should be isolated in a hospital cage. A flesh wound should be bathed in a mild antiseptic solution daily until it begins to heal. Broken leg bones may be repaired with a small splint and adhesive tape; wings may be set in

"Sick birds will often go off their food, and more often than not it is starvation that causes their death rather than the disease itself."

position by adhesive plaster alone. Such splints are left in position for six to eight weeks. In cases of profuse bleeding or extensive lacerations, a veterinarian should be consulted as soon as possible.

Overgrown Beak

An overgrown beak will occur if a bird has no access to items which it can chew at to keep the beak in trim. Most cockatiels are continually gnawing at something or other and the problem is rare. However, ensure that the birds have cuttlefish bone and twigs to chew at all times. Should the beak become overgrown it can be a major problem as it will come to a stage where the bird can no longer feed properly and, if untreated, starvation will result. An overgrown beak can be trimmed back to its normal shape using nail clippers or strong, sharp nail scissors. It is best to compare it with the beak of a normal bird while you are doing this. If you should accidentally cut into the blood supply while trimming the beak, the bleeding should be stopped as soon as possible with a styptic pencil or a little potash of alum.

Overgrown Nails

This is an affliction of birds which do not have adequate opportunities to exercise their feet and keep the claws worn to a reasonable length. The condition can be prevented by ensuring the birds have perches of varying thicknesses and textures. Natural perches are almost a necessity. If birds do get overgrown claws, they will become crippled and there is a danger of their getting caught in some part of the cage and injuring themselves. Claws can be trimmed to a reasonable length, using nail scissors or clippers. Hold the claw up to the light when doing this and you should be able to see the extent of the blood-vessel (the quick). Cut through the claw about 2mm ($1/8$ in) from the end of the quick. If you should accidentally cut into the blood supply, stop the bleeding as described above for beak trimming.

French Molt

There is currently little understanding of this

condition; it seems to happen among some stock but not others. Research is being conducted into the cause and treatment of the disease and it is hoped it will not be too long before we have conquered it. In French molt, fledging birds (usually) lose their flight and tail feathers and are thus unable to learn to fly. Such birds are often called infantrymen or runners. Less severely affected birds will eventually regrow their missing feathers but, in some cases, they remain missing and the birds are best humanely destroyed.

Get to know your cockatiel and check him out each and every day. This way you will quickly notice any change in his condition.

Eye Infections

These may be brought on by cold drafts and can be prevented by ensuring the birds have good, draft-proof sleeping quarters. A bird with a sore eye will rub it against a perch or with its foot. The eye will be reddened and the area around it will be inflamed; there will be a watery or yellowish discharge which will sometimes dry out and encrust the eyelids. Fortunately, most eye infections can be rapidly cured by bathing the eye with a mild antiseptic solution, then applying an eye ointment. Your veterinarian will advise you which products to use.

Respiratory Infections

These are caused by disease organisms of various types infecting the upper respiratory tract. Infected birds will cough and wheeze and the breathing will be labored. Birds suffering from stress through being kept in unsuitable conditions are most susceptible—damp and drafts being a major cause. Infected birds can soon infect other stock and

61

untreated respiratory infections can develop into fatal pneumonia. Sick birds should be removed to a warm hospital cage as soon as possible and treated as recommended by your veterinarian.

Bowel Infections

Diseases and conditions of the digestive canal are sometimes generally referred to as enteritis. However, there is a large number of different diseases which may infect various parts of the alimentary tract, plus a number of conditions which can be caused by an inadequate or too rich diet (too much greenfood of the wrong sort, for example, will result in non-infectious diarrhea). Infectious diseases of the bowel can be caused by bacteria, viruses or protozoa and are usually picked up by ingesting food which has been infected by the droppings of other birds (including wild birds) and vermin. Cleanliness of the cages, aviaries, food and utensils is an important prophylactic measure in the prevention of these diseases.

Crop trouble may occur occasionally in cockatiels, the crop becoming bloated and filled with frothy gas. The bird will retch and vomit and the feathers will become stained. The bird may be treated by holding it head downward and gently "milking" out the crop. A little potassium permanganate added to the drinking water, just enough to add a pink tinge, may help prevent such disorders. Intestinal enteritis is heralded by the bird looking distinctly sick and the presence of evil smelling, greenish or watery diarrhea which will stain the ventral area. Infected birds must be immediately isolated in a hospital cage and a veterinarian consulted. Many such diseases can be successfully treated with various drugs.

Endoparasites

These are parasites which live inside the body, and those that are likely to cause the majority of problems in cockatiels are various species of parasitic worms, including roundworms, threadworms and tapeworms. All of these worms live in the intestines of the bird and feed on partially digested

"Sick birds should be removed to a warm hospital cage as soon as possible and treated as recommended by your veterinarian."

food. Severe infestations of worms will take the nutrients from the bird before it can absorb them into its system and it will rapidly lose condition. The worms lay eggs in the intestines and these are passed out in the bird's droppings. If they find their way onto food materials, reinfection will occur continuously. Strict methods of hygiene, particularly with regard to feeding, will help keep worm infestations under control. Regular microscopic examinations (by a veterinary laboratory) will reveal any presence of worm eggs and indicate the species and degree of infestation. Proprietary worming compounds should be used according to the manufacturer's or veterinarian's instructions. After severe infestations, the aviary should be thoroughly disinfected to kill off any surviving eggs. The floor of the flight may be seared with a blowtorch and the turf, gravel or topsoil replaced.

Ectoparasites

There are a number of species of bloodsucking pests which can be classed as ectoparasites. They may infect the birds themselves, or the birds' quarters. Red mite, *Dermanyssus gallinae*, is fairly common and is usually carried to aviaries by wild birds. The mites live in cracks in nestboxes and in the aviary structure, coming out at night to feed on the roosting birds. Severe infestations will cause irritation, anemia and stress, which can result in a loss of resistance to other diseases. Infected birds will scratch themselves continually and appear to be in distress. Fortunately, red mite can be controlled by using one of the excellent miticides available on the market and used as per the manufacturer's instructions. Bird lice of various species may pose a problem occasionally but these can also be destroyed quite easily by using insecticidal dusts (of a type recommended for livestock). Regular cleaning and disinfecting of the aviary, nestboxes and other accessories, especially at the end of the breeding season, will help keep ectoparasites under control.

"Regular cleaning and disinfecting of the aviary, nestboxes and other accessories, especially at the end of breeding season, will help keep ectoparasites under control."

Index